Sunrise on the east wall of the Great House

AN ANCIENT TEMPLE. In 1890 Cosmos Mindeleff noted astutely that there was no problem giving the exact location of the Casa Grande, since "it is found easily by anyone looking for it."

Perched on top of the Great House, he described why: To the east the broad valley of the Gila River rises "in a great plain to a distant range of mountains. . . . On the northwest the valley of the Gila river runs into the horizon. . . . [T]oward the southwest and south it extends until in places it meets the horizon."

Mindeleff's sweeping description hints at why the builders may have chosen the site they did for construction of the four-story Casa Grande. The eye-stretching vistas afforded by the open-ness of the Gila River valley could have been advantageous for several reasons—detection of the approach of enemy raiders; observation of the canals that brought water to their fields; or perhaps a clear view of the heavens.

The United States government had directed Mr. Mindeleff to determine what repairs were needed to the "celebrated ruin of Casa Grande, an ancient temple of the prehistoric age." At the urging of a group of wealthy Bostonians, the govern-ment was preparing to reserve 480 acres to protect the ruin from the public that had already made its discovery and that was partly responsible for hastening its destruction.

Two years before Mindeleff's arrival, the youthful, colorful anthropologist, Frank Hamilton Cushing, had visited southern Arizona as head of the Hemenway Southwestern Archaeological Expedition. He was an instrumental figure in the action taken in 1892 that made Casa Grande the country's first archeological preserve.

Cushing, fresh from five years with the Zuni Indians of New Mexico, saw several parallels between Casa Grande and Zuni ceremonial structures. Like the kivas of the Zuni pueblos, the floorplan of the Great House was based on the four cardinal direc-tions—north, south, east, and west—and three additional domains of the native uni-verse—the zenith, nadir, and middle. Cushing went out on an archeological limb and proposed that the Great House had been a temple where high priests, like the rain priests at Zuni, had conducted religious ceremonies.

Today his speculations are gaining wider acceptance among archeologists such as Lynn Teague, who has done extensive work in the Salt-Gila region. She says that "the location of Casa Grande testifies, like its architecture, to a special role in large-scale social and economic institutions. . . .The Casa Grande is a classic example of a central place with respect to the middle Gila." Teague and others believe that full-time priests, or "ritual specialists," lived at Casa Grande, perhaps with their ex-tended families.

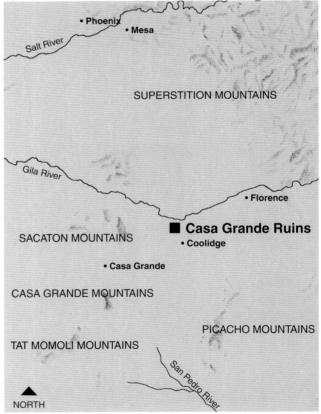

Mountain sheep effigy used for burning incense

Though other great houses may have existed, we do not yet have definite proof of them in the valleys of the Salt and Gila rivers, the heartland of a civilization of desert farmers known as the Hohokam.

The Hohokam lived in this region as long ago as A.D. 300 (the dates for the Hohokam period are subject to debate). During the earliest times, known as the Pioneer period, they built small settlements. Even in this initial stage they were digging irrigation canals and making pots and stone and shell goods. In the ensuing period, the Colonial, from about A.D. 550–700 to 950, the Hohokam expanded their range into tributaries of the Salt and Gila rivers. The Grewe site, a village a mile east of Casa Grande that was its predecessor, dates to this period. Important architectural traits, including ballcourts and platform mounds, appeared during the Colonial period. From about A.D. 950 to 1100 the Hohokam settled in, and their villages and hamlets grew steadily. This period has been termed the Sedentary, a time of almost mass production of artifacts with little innovation or experimentation.

Following the Sedentary, however, great changes have been documented. This period, known as the Classic, has brought unending speculation about the organization of Hohokam society. They turned to massive building, surrounding their villages and plazas with walls, digging huge pits, and erecting more platform mounds. One of the more tangible remains, their pottery, also shows signs that the status quo was somehow being altered.

Though the Great House itself was used for only about fifty to seventy-five years during the Classic period, it was part of a larger settlement complex, including the earlier Grewe site, that had existed for several centuries. The seeds of what the Casa Grande is believed to represent were planted much earlier at places like Grewe, which began to assume unusual importance among the Hohokam. At such sites, exotic luxuries and ritual paraphernalia are more prevalent than at other villages, and burials testify to the rise of an elite class. According to Lynn Teague, by A.D. 1300 changes had culminated in a new higher level of hierarchy, with the Casa Grande its ultimate expression.

T HE "HOTTAI—KI." Because it was so conspicuous the Great House was missed by few travelers and explorers. Fortunately, many of them wrote down their observations, giving us the benefit of 300 years of description and interpretation of the Casa Grande.

The government's emissary, Cosmos Mindeleff, scoured the historical accounts of those who had preceded him. He learned that the Casa Grande had been seen by Spaniards in the seventeenth century in the person of the great Jesuit padre, Father Eusebio Kino, who had trod many desert miles on horseback in search of converts to New Spain's empire. Father Kino was the first European to record the Casa Grande's existence.

Nearby Pima Indians already knew of it and had told Kino of a *hottai-ki*, or a Great House. With guides, he found what he called in his language the *casa grande*. To the Father it appeared "as large as a castle," unequaled by the largest churches in Sonora, Mexico. The year was 1694, and Father Kino, always aware of his higher mission, said mass within the walls of the ruin before sitting down to lunch.

Three years later Kino returned. With Captains Manje and Bernal and Indians and soldiers who joined along the way, they followed the San Pedro River to the Gila. At that time the Gila reportedly carried so much water that ships could navigate it. During this trip Manje and Bernal set down important descriptions of the Casa Grande, particularly of its construction. They noted that it was four stories high and that its thick walls were made with clay and mortar, "so smooth inside that they looked like brushed wood and so polished that they shone like Puebla earthenware." They also remarked on smaller houses around it and thought it clear that many people had lived there in a community.

Another man of the cloth, a Franciscan friar named Pedro Font, gave a report that especially interested Mindeleff. Font's description became the basis of nearly all the accounts written for the next century. On Halloween, 1775, Font wrote in his diary that his *comandante* had declared a day of rest on their journey from southern Arizona to California. Like Kino, Font had heard of the Great House from the Pimas. Instead of relaxing, he spent the day examining the ruin, measuring it with his lance and drawing it; he pronounced it an "oblong square. . .perfectly to the four winds." Observantly, he noted that the wood used in the ruin was pine and mesquite, and the only mountains where pine could be obtained were some "twenty and five leagues" distant.

The imaginations of future researchers would be stirred by another of Font's notations. In the walls of the Casa Grande were circular openings, some of which faced east and others west. According to the Pima Indians, these were

Aerial view of Casa Grande, ca. 1927

the openings through which "El Hombre Amargo," The Bitter Man, looked out and saluted the rising and setting sun.

Following in the footsteps of the Spanish explorers and missionaries seventy-five years later was the U. S. Army. Lieutenant William H. Emory, a topographical engineer with the Army of the West, saw the ruins during a lunch break on November 10, 1846. He and one of his staff, Captain A. R. Johnston, reported on the Casa Grande, its construction and size, as had those before them. They did, however, make an especially significant observation: some 200 yards from the Great House they spied a mound about 100 yards across,

hollow in the center, with ramps leading down to its floor, which Johnston thought was a partially filled well. This is believed to be the earliest record of a Hohokam ballcourt, an interesting feature that will receive more discussion later.

While waiting for the Pimas to bring him more mules, John Russell Bartlett, on a famous survey in 1852 to lay out the boundary line between the United States and Mexico, decided to take time to visit the "celebrated" Casa Grande ruin. Following the narrow ruts left six years earlier by a mountain howitzer, Bartlett traveled ten miles on a July day before he came to the building, its "bright walls" contrasting with the deep green of the

"mezquit" trees surrounding it. He stated correctly that the walls had been made of mud from the valley, but he incorrectly said that the builders had used forms to lay up the walls. Bartlett ventured a guess that corn had been stored in the inner rooms of the Casa Grande, and he raised the question of whether the entire edifice had been, in effect, a big silo.

At that early date he suggested optimistically that "a couple days labor" would be all that was necessary to restore the deteriorating walls, which were dissolving at their base due to moisture from the ground. Thus, the monument would be rendered "as durable as brick" and would last for centuries.

Early visitors stand in front of the Great House shortly after the first protective roof was built in 1903

Bartlett was off on his estimate of what it would take to preserve and protect the Casa Grande, but he was right on another point: the Great House, exposed as it was to the raw elements, was suffering badly from the vagaries of weathering.

CARETAKING THE CURIOSITIES. What John Russell Bartlett and others had seen in the mid-nineteenth century was only becoming worse by the time Cosmos Mindeleff was sent on his inspection. The walls of the Casa Grande were fissured and huge chunks were collapsing. Sapping of groundwater up through the earth was undermining its base. Another form of destruction was also threatening. By the end of the 1800s, Casa Grande was becoming well-known among travelers. Early explorers and visitors felt compelled to scrawl their names on the plaster of the inner walls and to pilfer pottery, roof beams, door lintels, and anything else that wasn't tied down.

J. Ross Browne, with one group of visitors, said they left after a day at the ruin "well laden with curiosities. Every member of the party had his fragment of pottery and specimen of adobe and plaster." By the time Mindeleff saw the Casa Grande in 1890, he had to report that tourists had "torn out and carried away every lintel and every particle of visible wood in the building."

Inscriptions on the walls, though certainly defacing, paradoxically are nuggets of historical interest. For instance, Sheldon Jackson, a Presbyterian minister known to his admirers as "The Great Bishop of the Great Beyond," left his name, as did California '49er H.B. Summers, who later settled in Florence, Arizona. One inscription, that of "P. Weaver 183___," has provoked speculation. Though the exact year and the first name are uncertain, this is generally said to be the handiwork of Pauline Weaver, a mountain man known to have roamed Arizona in the 1830s.

John Rockfellow, a New Yorker turned Westerner, in a letter to park officials in 1935, wrote that he and his partner, Bill Hartt, had stopped by Casa Grande on their way to Tombstone and a supposed mining bonanza. He admitted that he used a small prospector's pick to chip his fraternity insignia on the walls of the ruin. Hartt, the taller of the two, inscribed his trademark—a heart with eyes, nose, and mouth—above Rockfellow's sign.

One reason for the onslaught of visitors to Casa Grande in the 1880s was completion of the Southern Pacific Railroad to Tucson. A station was located at the town of Casa Grande, only twenty miles from the ruin. By 1912, the year Arizona gained statehood, daily stage

trips were being run between the ruin and its namesake town. The fifty-mile round trip cost five dollars a person, with a three-hour stopover so visitors could tour the Casa Grande.

By this time the Casa Grande had been sheltered under a roof put in place in 1903. The roof and repairs to the structure—which included clearing away rubbish, bracing and underpinning the walls, replacing lintels, and filling holes—were a result of the report that Mindeleff filed. In addition, an important federal law, the "Antiquities Act," had been passed in 1906 that made it illegal to remove materials or deface prehistoric sites.

One man—Frank Pinkley—was perhaps most responsible for recognition of Casa Grande. The first custodian to live at the ruins, Pinkley spent twenty-seven years interpreting Casa Grande to a growing number of visitors, while fulfilling his bureaucratic duties and encouraging archeologists to study it.

At age twenty Frank Pinkley took his new bride, Edna Townsley, to live in a frame-sided tent pitched in a mesquite grove in the shadow of the Great House. They drew their water from a well that Pinkley dug, and later, with their own money, built an adobe house at the ruins.

In 1915, frustrated with Congress's failure to appropriate money for the monument, he left his job to join the state legislature. Three years later, Pinkley resumed his position at Casa Grande, at the astounding salary of $990 a year, under the condition that the National Park Service would furnish a car

for which he would buy the gas.

The Model T Ford (that the Pinkleys named "Baby") took the couple all over the Southwest, as Frank discharged his duties at other monuments, in addition to Casa Grande. Ninety-two thousand miles later, "Baby" was regretfully retired, but not without a special "Ode to the Old Ford" given in eulogy.

Pinkley dutifully reported each month to his superior, Stephen Mather, director of the newly created National Park Service. These monthly narrations concerned themselves with visitation, finances, maintenance and labor matters, the weather, general business and farming conditions in the area, and any other details Pinkley thought would interest Mr. Mather.

In 1919 he happily announced that a telephone had been installed at the

monument, eliminating a day's delay in getting messages. As a continuing sign of the strides being made in transportation and communication in the world, Pinkley informed Mather the following year that "on the afternoon of the 9th an aeroplane passed over the monument on its way from Tucson to Phoenix."

The increasing mobility of Americans was also being felt at Casa Grande National Monument, and Pinkley tried to keep pace. His aim was to have personal contact with every visitor, admitting in his February 1926 report to Mather that office work had fallen behind because he and one other employee had received 1,416 visitors at the Casa Grande. They had worked every day that month, "Sundays being the heaviest days of travel." A month earlier, reconstruction of the new museum had just been completed, necessary because a flood the previous fall had destroyed it.

Nineteen twenty-six proved to be a busy year at Casa Grande. In November the monument hosted a pageant of ambitious proportions. It featured a play, complete with "weird tribal dances and chants, pipes of priest," tom-toms, and wailing women, wrote Frank Russell in "Progressive Arizona." The second act promised "real Indians in the flesh," and the grand finale would be a raising of voices in the hymn, "Oh God, Our Help in Ages Past." The pageant would, in Mr. Russell's mind, inaugurate a "new era in the artistic life of Arizona." The production was staged next to the Great House on Compound B at sunset. Thirteen thousand people attended, with seating provided for only a fourth that number.

Despite its apparent initial success, what pageant promoters had hoped would become an annual event was discontinued four years later.

Amid his work of publicizing Casa Grande and digging into its archeology, Pinkley's utmost priority was protecting the monument from vandalism and disintegration. He took up where Mindeleff and others left off in attempts to stabilize and preserve the ruin.

The earliest stabilization work at Casa Grande, from the years 1889 to 1907, involved largely structural reinforcement and measures to halt erosion at the bases of the walls. In 1891, Jesse Walter Fewkes, marine biologist turned

southwestern archeologist, came to assess its condition. In 1906 and 1907 he engaged in excavation and stabilization work. Among other things, Fewkes cemented the lower walls and dug drainage ditches to divert runoff from Compound A.

The use of cement as a cap to prevent erosion gained favor for several years, until about 1932. Then for a brief period a wave of research and experimentation commenced to find a resin or waterproofing substance that would save the walls of the Casa Grande. The park service received many responses to its request for suggestions for preservatives, including one from a Los Angeles

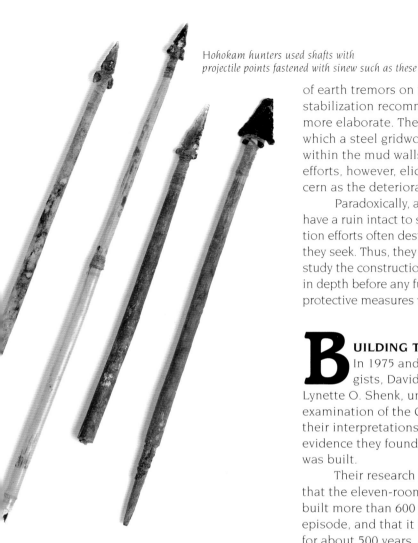

of earth tremors on the Casa Grande, and stabilization recommendations became more elaborate. They suggested a plan in which a steel gridwork would be epoxied within the mud walls. Such radical efforts, however, elicited as much concern as the deterioration itself.

Paradoxically, archeologists must have a ruin intact to study it, but preservation efforts often destroy the very evidence they seek. Thus, they asked for time to study the construction of the Casa Grande in depth before any further stabilization or protective measures were taken.

BUILDING THE GREAT HOUSE.

In 1975 and 1976, two archeologists, David R. Wilcox and Lynette O. Shenk, undertook a detailed examination of the Great House and gave their interpretations, based on the evidence they found, of when and how it was built.

Their research led them to conclude that the eleven-room Casa Grande was built more than 600 years ago, in a single episode, and that it had been abandoned for about 500 years. And the people who built it had a definite floorplan in mind.

To build the Casa Grande, the Hohokam used what was handiest—mud. Especially, they took advantage of the lime-rich caliche that is found several feet below the sandy ground. Caliche, known for good reasons as "hardpan," is clay and sand with a heavy dose of calcium carbonate. When solidified underground, it has the consistency of concrete. Metal shovels cannot dent it, and experienced desert dwellers know

that the only way to soften caliche is to add water. The Hohokam must have discovered this early on.

The caliche was "puddled" in small mixing pits dug into the ground. After softened to the consistency of a good mud pie, it could be kneaded into a stiff dough. It was then laid up in courses about two feet high, without benefit of forms or other structures to hold it upright while it dried. The method is known as "English cob;" though some have called the material adobe, technically it is not. Jesse Fewkes commented that at various places on the walls of Compound A, in which the Casa Grande is located, the imprints of human hands could still be seen where the mud was patted into shape.

Early historical accounts were in disagreement over whether the Casa Grande was three or four stories high. The confusion may have resulted from the fact that the ground floor had been

inventor whose letterhead listed cures for gallstone and consumption, hair growers, and synthetic milk, among an impressively long litany. Nothing materialized from the search, however, so it was back to the old standby, cement.

According to monument archeologist Charlie Steen, the results of the various experiments showed that cement breaks and cracks, and sprays "do more harm than good." By the 1970s engineers had expressed concern about the effects filled in and was actually the base for the other three stories. The Pinkleys believed that the Hohokam filled in the bottom floor so that the four-foot-thick walls, standing thirty to forty-five feet high, could be adequately supported. Wilcox and Shenk say that evidence strongly supports the inference that the building still stands at about its original height.

Study of the wood used in the Casa Grande reinforces the suggestion that the Hohokam were intent on building a grand edifice. Five species of wood were used as beams: ponderosa pine, juniper, white fir, mesquite, and a fifth "nonconifer," possibly cottonwood. Juniper, pine and fir are not available locally, and the closest place to get them would have meant a journey to mountains at least fifty miles away.

After the people had traveled to get the wood, they somehow had to get it back to the building site. The logs might have been rafted down the Gila River, but no signs of water wear could be detected on the samples. The ends of the beams, which are all that remain now, appear to have been cut with a stone axe. Some 640 beams, of fairly uniform lengths, were used in the Casa Grande, each as heavy as a twelve-foot-long two-by-four. If the beams had to be carried in on someone's back, we begin to gain an idea of how badly they wanted the wood. The alternative to wood-harvesting expeditions could have been trade, though the trouble of transporting the beams remains.

However they were obtained, back at the building site the wooden beams were placed across the room spaces,

plastered down with mud, and laid over with saguaro ribs or reeds perpendicular to the main beams. This lattice affair was then covered with bundles of grassy reeds or cane, and wet mud served as a final sealer. Impressions of the reeds and saguaro ribs can still be seen in many of the walls in the Casa Grande.

The beams hold potential importance for another reason—determining the age of the Casa Grande. In the Southwest the annual growth rings on

trees allow wood samples from archeological sites to be dated to a specific year. Tree-rings vary in width depending on the amount of rainfall. Over time, the rings show a pattern that can be compared with a master set of tree-rings. However, the wood used at Casa Grande that would furnish the best tree-ring dates, the white fir, has not been found in large enough pieces to allow its dating.

Dates have been obtained by park service archeologist John Andresen using

radiocarbon dating, which measures the amount of carbon 14, based on its known decay rate, in organic material. Radiocarbon dates on beam samples from Casa Grande indicate that it was constructed during the early-1300s, which agrees with other relative dates.

How long did it take to build the Casa Grande? Wilcox and Shenk tried to answer this question by estimating time and number of people involved. In their opinion, neither an extremely large work force nor a "terribly sophisticated social structure" was required to build it. No doubt there was a boss, and possibly an architect was in charge. And someone had to organize the workers to get wood, if in fact that was done, and to inspire them to keep mixing the caliche and laying up the walls.

Making some assumptions about volume of material and number of trips back and forth, they calculated that twenty-four people could "easily" have built the walls of the Casa Grande in a year. A hundred people—perhaps twenty-five families—could have accomplished it in three months (assuming that our modern eight-hour workday was in effect and child labor laws were not!)

Was the Casa Grande well built? Cosmos Mindeleff did not think it represented exceptional workmanship, citing the uneven thicknesses of the walls and crooked floor joists. Civil engineer Henry Hillman, on the other hand, writing nearly a century after Mindeleff, was "very impressed" with the square corners, the close lengths of the opposite sides, and the horizontal door and window lintels. In his view, "Compared to many other ruins in Arizona, this structure is outstanding from an engineering viewpoint."

What impressed him even more was his finding of a common unit of measure used in the Casa Grande. Hillman calls it the megalithic yard, equal to about 2.75 to 2.80 feet. Applying to the Casa Grande, he shows the building to be nearly a perfect 3:4 rectangle with a diagonal of 5, indicating to him that while its builders may not have been conscientious in their choice of floor joists, they possibly had knowledge of and were able to apply the Pythagorean theorem.

Another revelation about the architecture of the Great House casts light on its possible use, a question that to this day remains an enigma. On the summer solstice each year an intriguing

event occurs at the Casa Grande. At sunset through a round window in an upper story wall, the sun aligns between two edges of the window, leading some people to believe that the opening was purposefully placed to provide a sort of calendar for the people of Casa Grande.

Archaeoastronomy, the term that has been applied to this study of celestial events at archeological sites, is gaining fans throughout the Southwest and elsewhere. Whether Casa Grande is on the same footing as England's Stonehenge, as some have suggested, is open to question. It seems reasonable, however, that the oval, circular, and rectangular openings in certain parts of the building may have been intentionally placed to serve special purposes. Perhaps they really were the openings through which "Bitter Man" saluted the rising and setting sun.

After taking compass readings on all the ports in the upper rooms of the Casa Grande in 1970 and 1971, John Molloy concluded that the Great House may have been used for viewing or predicting a number of astronomical events, including solstices, equinoxes, and eclipses. The careful sizing of the openings suggested to him that a conscious effort had been made to meet predetermined guidelines. He found the Round Window an "impressively accurate" solstice indicator. Further, he thought that the knowledge and sophistication necessary to make these sorts of observations indicated the existence of an elite priesthood.

The idea of sun holes, or calendar holes, at Casa Grande goes back at least to 1918, when Frank Pinkley mentioned to Stephen Mather that the holes on the second floor formed a sort of clock. These

particular openings have been debunked by later research which showed them to be tie rod holes drilled during stabilization in 1891. The upper-room holes that Molloy and others have studied, however, were constructed differently and are prehistoric.

OF BALLCOURTS AND BURIALS. Although the Great House can not help but be the focus of so much attention, if for no other reason than its dominance over the scene, a number of other features have been discovered in the vicinity that tell us more about the Hohokam—how they lived, how they died, and what they valued.

Recall Captain Johnston, who accompanied Lieutenant Emory in 1846: he saw, not 200 yards from the Casa Grande, a depression with mounded sides that he surmised was a partially filled well. His mention of that feature would lead to an intriguing line of research about what are now considered to be courts upon which the Hohokam played some sort of ballgame.

There have been, however, as many interpretations of this and similar depressions as there have been observers. Surveyor John Russell Bartlett thought the one at Casa Grande was a stock corral; archeologists Adolph Bandelier and Jesse Walter Fewkes believed it was a reservoir or tank; and Frank Hamilton Cushing called it a "sun temple," some kind of ceremonial chamber. Cosmos Mindeleff expressed uncertainty. He did not hold to the reservoir idea, though were the depression not so deep it could have been a grain threshing floor, he suggested.

Frank Pinkley, who tended to agree with Cushing, decided to test these possibilities. The reservoir idea did not appeal to Pinkley because the sides of the mound had been built about eight feet above the desert floor. After discussing the features in one of his monthly reports to Mather, Pinkley dug around a bit in the mysterious pit and others nearby.

In one, he found a packed caliche floor that sloped upward to the dirt banks, and in the middle of the floor he located a hard green stone. Under the center stone in the floor of another mound he uncovered a cache of shell and a turquoise bangle. Pinkley proposed to Mather that the park service garner some publicity from the results of his investigations and then allow scientists to excavate.

Sixty-three years later, researcher David Wilcox launched an extensive study of ballcourts throughout the Salt-Gila region, including the court at Casa Grande. Influenced by archeologist Emil Haury's acceptance that a ballcourt had indeed been uncovered at nearby Snaketown, plus the weight of other such discoveries in the Southwest, Wilcox argues that the so-called "bowls" or "mounds" were courts for playing ballgames like those documented in Mexico and in the Maya area. In Mexico the ball, most likely made of natural rubber from a plant, was knocked through stone rings high on the walls of the court. The players, at least in the Mesoamerican matches, wore shields to protect their bodies. To make the game more challenging, they could hit the ball with hips, knees, or elbows, but not their hands or feet. Wilcox and others think that the Hohokam probably adapted their courts to local conditions and played a similar game.

Other evidence supports archeologist Edwin Ferdon's idea that the ballcourt was a dance platform. These various interpretations may not be mutually exclusive, points out one of his colleagues, and like so much in archeology may simply be a function of several people "feeling different parts of the elephant."

The Casa Grande ballcourt is one of some 200 courts known in the Southwest, and it may have been one of the latest ones built. Some 300 to 600 people could have circled the sides of the court to watch the game, perhaps wagering on the home team in a prehistoric version of Monday night football.

The ballcourt at Snaketown, a nearby Hohokam site

In Wilcox's opinion, the games may have helped settle disputes, aided in redistributing goods, or perhaps held ceremonial symbolism for the Hohokam. The way that ballcourts are distributed along major drainages in the Phoenix Basin, in which Casa Grande Monument is located, argues to him that they may have been part of a widely distributed village network.

Besides their ballcourts, there is much about the Hohokam that shows a great sense of playfulness. Their jewelry, pottery, shell and stonework designs—with flying birds, running mammals, and twined snakes—are especially whimsical and lively. Delicate shellwork is one of their trademarks. Much of the shell they worked came from the Gulf of California, so trade or shell-gathering expeditions undoubtedly were involved. On the shell, they incised, sculpted, and engraved

frogs, birds, snakes, and human forms. Geometric shapes later came into vogue. Elaborate mosaics of inlaid turquoise may have demanded a specialist's expertise. Some shell was made into rings, bracelets, and beads, while others were simply made in the likeness of common animals.

One imaginative method of etching shell apparently is unique to the Hohokam. Emil Haury tried it himself and it works. The shell was bathed in fermented saguaro juice, acting as an acid, that dissolved parts of the shell that had not been coated with a resistant wax or pitch; thus a design was created in relief.

Hohokam artisans could also satisfy their creative urges through pottery-making, a skill that showed their penchant for elaborate, distinct designs, and that, unbeknownst to them, would furnish an indispensable record of their lives to future archeologists.

The single pottery type that best identifies the Classic period, known as Casa Grande Red-on-Buff, was manufactured into several forms: jars, bowls, and pitchers, among them. The pots were constructed of coils of clay wound one on top of the other, and thinned and

Hohokam carved slate figurine

Bounty of the desert: creosote bush (foreground), ironwood tree, and saguaro cactus

smoothed with a wooden paddle. The paste was pink to light tan, with a light buff slip on the outside of the pot, tempered with a quartz-based material. Using the tip of a cactus spine, or perhaps a chewed twig, a woman would paint solid lines, curves, and triangles in maroon or light orange on the outside of a pot. In a hot mesquite or ironwood fire the pots gained a hard, durable finish.

Hohokam pottery began to change during the Classic period. Jars, previously made with low shoulders and sharply turned rims, were made rounder, with taller necks. Designs became simpler, and by the end of the period Casa Grande Red-on-Buff was rarely found. Not as much painted pottery was produced, and what was made was smaller and lacked the artful designs and crisp patterns. Instead, design was achieved by

smokeblackened smudges on the insides of the pots. Interestingly, another completely different pottery style—Gila Poly-chrome—emerged.

Gila Polychrome originated in the region north and east of the Hohokam, but the style was widespread and has been found far south in Mexico. Snake and bird designs were common, painted in red, white, and black. The presence of Gila Polychrome in archeological sites is significant for dating, since it is a marker for the year 1300 and beyond, the last years of the Classic period. And it represents a new idea entering Hohokam life.

While it is certainly more pleasant to dwell on the lighter side of Hohokam life, some of the more tangible evidence we have of their society is their burials. Unlike the two other major southwestern cultures, the Anasazi and the Mogollon, the Hohokam cremated their dead and buried the ashes and any remaining bones in urns and pits in the ground. Later, they began to bury some bodies in the ground, and whole skeletons have been unearthed. Jewelry, tools, pottery, and sometimes clothing have been found with burials. The method of burial, accompanying items, and analysis of the bones tells us a good deal about the people—their sex, age, and health condition, and their possible status in the community.

Harold Gladwin located twenty-

seven cremation burials outside Compound B at Casa Grande and two skeletons, one of which was judged to be an elderly person because the bones showed signs of rheumatism. In another place Richard Ambler counted thirty-two cremations; with the bones and ashes were potsherds, bowls, a scoop, and a plate. Two of the burials were identified: one was a twenty-five year old female, the other was a child, seven to twelve years old.

Also, patterns have been detected in burial practices: certain people were buried in special places with prized possessions accompanying them. Jesse Walter Fewkes, in his early twentieth-century excavations at Casa Grande, uncovered a burial in a room of what he called Clan House A. It was the skeleton of an old man, fully extended, with the head pointing east. With it was a recep-tacle that held a grooved double-edged axe, paint grinder and pestle, and a "medicine outfit" that contained several different pigments. All of this Fewkes interpreted as "priestly paraphernalia," and he believed the man had been an important chief.

GRASSROOTS.

GRASSROOTS. The Hohokam were, first and foremost, farmers. While the chiefs may have resided in the cool rooms of the Casa Grande, the average Hohokam was out sweating in the dusty fields. Their arid environment led them to employ several strategies, including dry farming, floodwater farming, and irrigation. They were masters of irrigated agriculture, and their waterways, dug by hand with stone tools, were even reused by later European settlers.

A major canal that heads on the Gila River about sixteen miles above Casa Grande, with side canals sprouting off it, brought the necessary water to their fields. From the top story of the Great House they could keep constant vigil on the canals, the virtual lifelines of their existence.

Monument employee Frank Midvale spent many years searching for signs of prehistoric agriculture around Casa Grande. By 1965 he was able to relocate only eight of eighty-five miles of major canals identified in the early 1900s. What Midvale found were "inconspicuous remains," unnoticeable to a casual observer since they had long been eroded or buried by blowing sand.

He pinpointed them by carefully observing slight depressions or a path of stone tools that marked a canal course.

Some that he was able to measure were twenty-five to forty feet from bank to bank. The Hohokam, Midvale thought, built dikes of brush and sand to divert water from the river. After experience with frequent washouts, they combined several small canals with a common heading, thus strengthening the system.

The Hohokam's command of irrigation's finer points—solving problems of intakes, finding the best routes, and locating fields advantageously—indicated that they learned quickly from their experiences. As Emil Haury has said, "The evidences we are privileged to study tend to show the Hohokam did mostly the right things." But like people everywhere, "they had troubles, and they must have made mistakes."

Haury found that the extensive canal system at Snaketown, downstream

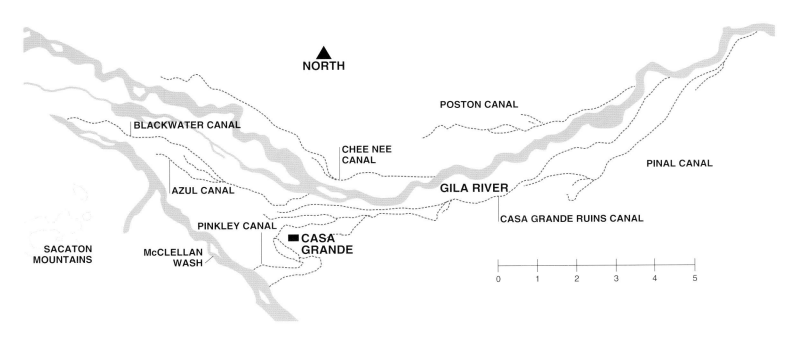

The extensive canal system built by the Hohokam

on the Gila River from Casa Grande, showed a complex overlapping of ditches and evidence of remodeling. No doubt the same type of maintenance had to be performed at Casa Grande.

Some higher level of organization likely was necessary to insure that the irrigation system worked. Canal maintenance had to be coordinated because the work of one group downstream would be in vain if others upstream were not doing the same. In addition, some sort of regulation of water supply would have been necessary during low-water periods. Those at the end of the pipe, so to speak, would want assurance that water would reach them at critical times during the growing season. Features called platform mounds may have provided the necessary connections that ensured smooth working of the irrigation systems. Hohokam researcher David Gregory mapped platform mounds in the Salt and Gila river valleys, and noted a regular distribution of them along major canals. At Casa Grande and at five sites upriver Gregory identified platform mounds at evenly spaced intervals along two major canals.

As had others before him, Gregory observed that these platform mounds began to look alike and became widespread during the Classic period. They consistently were built with rectangular retaining walls, filled with trash or soil, and then capped to form a hard surface. The Hohokam placed structures on top of the mounds, enclosed the mounds with compound walls, and then apparently lived there. The people who occupied the mounds during the Classic possibly were those who held power; they may have overseen the workers who built the mounds and ballcourts and maintained the canals.

In their irrigated fields the Hohokam grew corn, beans, squash, cotton, and tobacco. Corn, especially, was a staple of their diets. The corn, or maize, had evolved over thousands of years from a wild grass of Mexico into a race that was cold-and drought-resistant. The Hohokam possibly could have planted two crops each year—one in early spring and another in late summer.

Early races of corn were not like our familiar Iowa-grown varieties. The cobs were small and the kernels grew in gnarled rows. The Hohokam raised mostly popcorn and flour corn, although they possibly had sweet corn, too. Whole kernels were parched or ground into flour used to bake bread. From the roofs of their houses they may have strung ears of corn for later use. Beans, including common frijoles and a variety popular among the Pima and Papago, the tepary, were the second most important cultivated crop. Squash completed the sacred crop triumvirate and, most important, furnished an amino acid, tryptophan, not present in corn.

Ethnobotanists, who study the plant uses of native people, also think that the Hohokam encouraged weeds like purslane, pigweed, and mustard to grow among the rows of corn and beans.

Ripe red fruit of the Saguaro

Bighorn sheep were prized but hard to come by

These, too, were gathered and eaten, and were surprisingly nutritious.

The Hohokam knew better than to rely totally on what they could grow by the sweat of their brows and the wishes of the gods. To supplement their cultivated foods, they enjoyed the bounty of the desert. Just as the spring corn harvest was running low in July, the saguaro cactus that grows on the hillsides offered up its crimson fruits. They used the fruit to its fullest—cooking the pulp into juice or wine and eating the leftover black seeds. By September, pods of mesquite and screwbean, trees that were once abundant along the Gila, could be gathered and ground into meal. The sweet, succulent innards of agave stems were also highly sought, and agave may have been cultivated for food.

Dependent as they were on weather and, by our standards, crude farming methods, the Hohokam could not afford to be gourmets. They ate nearly anything they could get their hands on—including birds, jackrabbits, lizards and snakes, fish and a mule deer or bighorn sheep if they were lucky enough to find one. They roasted or broiled a good deal of their meat, or baked it in earthen ovens. During hard times, though, they didn't bother. They simply ate the food raw, bones and all.

on control of canal systems or changes in trade networks.

Though the Hohokam undertook during the Classic to build platform mounds and more massive buildings like the Casa Grande, their pottery and other art forms tell us the sparks of original creativity had cooled.

THE END, OR WAS IT? No signs of the Hohokam have been found that date beyond the year A.D. 1450. About 1350, population began to decline, and though people still lived at Casa Grande, they returned to simpler structures. Platform mounds and public architecture, such as the Casa Grande, were no longer part of the scene, during this post-Classic period. The Hohokam had lived in this desert successfully for more than a thousand years, and archeologists still cannot say with certainty what brought about their demise. Baffling questions remain.

Why was the Casa Grande, which apparently had taken a concerted effort to build, abandoned in such a relatively short time? Recent evidence points to a drastic flood around 1350 that perhaps destroyed their irrigation canals and thus the basis of their economy.

As is almost always the case, the stage had already been set in an earlier time. Early in Classic period, Hohokam population apparently increased, which meant more mouths to feed and perhaps a more elaborate social system to produce more food. A high priest or authority figure would have been needed to keep things on track. Their society changed from an egalitarian one to one marked by increased specialization and centralization. Also during this time alliances with the region may have formed, dissolved, and reformed, based

The purpose of the Casa Grande itself during this time is still a question. A refuge in an emergency, perhaps? If the Hohokam were growing more corn, they might have needed a very large storage place for it; or if priests did in fact govern, the Great House might have served as a sacred "temple" or watchtower from which they could proclaim seasonal observances to the masses. They and their families might even have lived there.

Tightly coiled pods of the screwbean mesquite

The Great House   25

Hohokam artifacts from left: bone awl on sharpening stone, slate used for sharpening, and arrow with projectile point on a double shaft straightening and smoothing stone

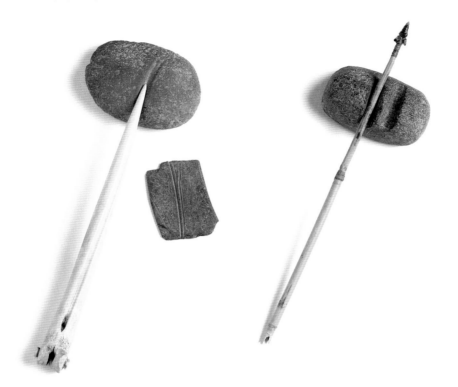

Harold S. Gladwin, among the first to define the Hohokam in the 1930s, believed that "back of it all is the feeling that, in one way or another, we are seeking the truth, and that someday, out of all our conflicting theories, a story can be told which will be convincingly true."

"Hohokam" means "used up," or by some definitions "those who have perished or vanished." We do not know what happened to them, but while they were here they built a fascinating settlement at Casa Grande, dominated by a structure that remains as mysterious as their demise.

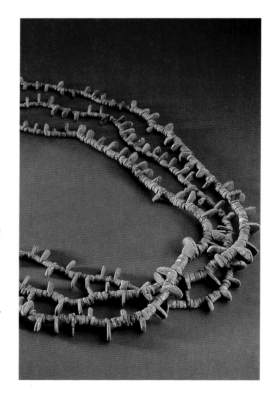

Its uniqueness has made the Casa Grande a symbol of the Classic period of the Hohokam. The enormous changes that were occurring, including the entry of outsiders into the Hohokam region, have led some to ask whether it was actually the Hohokam who built the Casa Grande. They consider it typical of pueblo-type dwellings, introduced by the same people who may also have been responsible for the changes in pottery style and burial practices.

Two possible links to the Hohokam are the modern Pima Indians, who were living in brush huts in the Gila Valley when Father Kino visited the ruins of Casa Grande in 1694, and the Tohono O'odham whose reservation lies west of Tucson. Whether they are the direct descendants of the Hohokam is another question that begs more study. Still others believe that the Hohokam became an extinct people.

Archeologists may be able to learn exactly when and why the Casa Grande was built, and they may satisfactorily resolve the difficult question of abandonment. With the time-tested technique of the shovel (and now with computers, backhoes, and sophisticated dating tools) they may be able to tell us the answers.

Hohokam turquoise necklace

Turquoise and hematite mosaic earrings such as these may have been a valuable trade item for the Hohokam

READINGS

Ambler, J. Richard. "An Archaeological Survey of Casa Grande National Monument, Arizona" *The Kiva*, Vol. 27, No. 4, 1962.

Fewkes, Jesse Walter. Casa Grande, Arizona. *28th Annual Report of the Bureau of American Ethnology*. Washington, D.C. 1906—07, 1912.

Gladwin, Harold S. "Excavations at Casa Grande, Arizona." *Southwest Museum, Papers 2*, Los Angeles: Southwest Museum, 1928.

Gladwin, Harold S., Emil W. Haury, E. B. Sayles, and Nora Gladwin. *Excavations at Snaketown: Material Culture*. Tucson: University of Arizona Press, 1965.

Gregory, David A. "The Morphology of Platform Mounds and the Structure of Classic Period Hohokam Sites," paper presented at the Forty-seventh Annual Meeting of the Society for American Archaeology, Minneapolis: April, 1982.

Gumerman, George J., and Emil W. Haury. "Prehistory: Hohokam." in *Handbook of North American Indians*, Vol 9. Washington, D. C.: Smithsonian Institution, 1979. University of Arizona Press in collaboration with Southwest Parks and Monuments Association, 1976.

Haury, Emil W. *The Hohokam: Desert Farmers & Craftsmen*. Tucson: University of Arizona Press in collaboration with Southwest Parks and Monuments Association, 1976.

Midvale, Frank. "Prehistoric Irrigation of the Casa Grande Ruin Area." *The Kiva*, Vol. 30, No. 3, February 1965.

Mindeleff, Cosmos. Casa Grande Ruin. *13th Annual Report of the Bureau of American Ethnology*. Washington, D. C., 1896.

Steen, Charlie R. "Excavations in Compound A, Casa Grande National Monument, 1963." *The Kiva*, Vol. 31, No. 2, December 1965.

Teague, Lynn S., and Patricia L. Crown. *Hohokam Archeology Along the Salt Gila Aqueduct, Central Arizona Project*. Vol. 9, Synthesis and Conclusions. Tucson: Arizona State Museum, Archaeological Series No. 150, 1984.

Van Valkenburg, Sallie. "The Casa Grande of Arizona as a Landmark on the Desert, A Government Reservation, and a National Monument." *The Kiva*, Vol. 27, No. 3, February 1962.

Wilcox, David R. *The Relationship of Casa Grande Ruin to Compound A: Research Potential of the in situ Deposits*. Tucson: Arizona State Museum, Archaeological Series No. 83, 1975.

Wilcox, David R., and Lynette O. Shenk. *The Architecture of the Casa Grande and Its Interpretation*. Tucson: Arizona State Museum, Archaeological Series No. 115, 1977.

Wilcox, David R., and Charles Sternberg. *Hohokam Ballcourts and Their Interpretation*. Tucson: Arizona State Museum, Archaeological Series No. 160, 1983.

ACKNOWLEDGMENTS

An author is always indebted to many people for any writing effort, and this one is no different. I want to thank John Andresen, staff archeologist at Casa Grande Ruins National Monument, and Superintendent Donald L. Spencer for help during my research and for review of the manuscript. David Wilcox and David Gregory patiently tried to educate me about the Hohokam and the fascinating results of their research. Staff at the National Park Service's Western Archeological and Conservation Center, in particular Keith Anderson and Anne Trinkle Jones, were most helpful, as was Tanner Pilley with the Southern Arizona Group of the NPS. Lynn Teague of the Arizona State Museum made many valuable comments to the draft manuscript, as did Bernard Fontana and David Lavender. Finally, I thank T. J. Priehs of Southwest Parks and Monuments Association for his unflagging support and understanding, not to mention his lucid and always needed editorial critique.

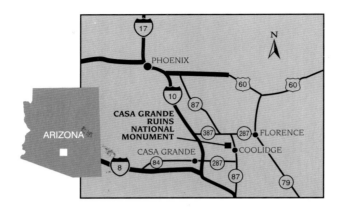

Second Edition
Copyright © 1996 by Southwest Parks and Monuments Association, Tucson, Arizona

ISBN: 1-877856-71-1
Library of Congress Number: 96-70558

Written by Rose Houk
Edited by Laura Symms-Wallace
Designed by Rita Ellsworth
Illustrations by Lawrence Ormsby
Photography by George H. H. Huey, cover, pages 3, 4, 5, 15 (bowl), 16 (hedgehog), 19, 20 (jar), 22 (saguaro); Jerry Jacka, pages 10, 12-14, 15 (pins)
courtesy Gerold Collins, 16 (portal), 18, 20 (bowl) courtesy Dennis and Janis Lyon, 26 (necklace courtesy Arizona State Museum), 27;
Patrick Fischer, page 11; Tom Danielsen, page 25; and Mark Thaler, pages 23-24.
Historic photos courtesy Arizona State Museum, The University of Arizona, page 17 by Emil Haury, 22 by Helga Teiwes; Casa Grande Ruins
National Monument, 7-9 (Ruins photo by Henry C. Peabody); and Western Archeological and Conservation Center in Tucson, page 6 by Neil Judd.
Map (back cover) by Triad and Associates
Printing by Arizona Lithographers

Artifacts shown in this publication are not from known burial sites.

Net proceeds from the sale of SPMA publications support
educational and scientific activities in the National Park System.